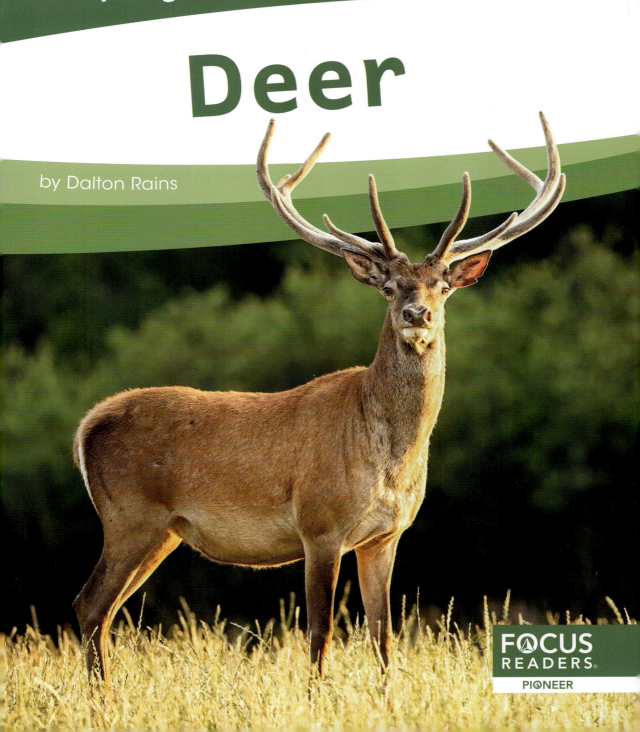

Neighborhood Safari

Deer

by Dalton Rains

www.focusreaders.com

Copyright © 2025 by Focus Readers®, Mendota Heights, MN 55120. All rights reserved. No part of this book may be reproduced or utilized in any form or by any means without written permission from the publisher.

Focus Readers is distributed by North Star Editions: sales@northstareditions.com | 888-417-0195

Produced for Focus Readers by Red Line Editorial.

Photographs ©: Shutterstock Images, cover, 1, 4, 6, 8, 10, 12, 15, 17, 18, 21

Library of Congress Cataloging-in-Publication Data
Names: Rains, Dalton, author.
Title: Deer / by Dalton Rains.
Description: Mendota Heights, MN: Focus Readers, [2025] | Series: Neighborhood safari | Includes bibliographical references and index. | Audience: Grades K-1
Identifiers: LCCN 2023056269 (print) | LCCN 2023056270 (ebook) | ISBN 9798889981749 (hardcover) | ISBN 9798889982302 (paperback) | ISBN 9798889983415 (pdf) | ISBN 9798889982869 (ebook)
Subjects: LCSH: Deer--Juvenile literature | Deer--Anatomy--Juvenile literature | Deer--Behavior--Juvenile literature | Deer--Life cycles--Juvenile literature
Classification: LCC QL737.U55 R35 2025 (print) | LCC QL737.U55 (ebook) | DDC 599.65--dc23/eng/20240102
LC record available at https://lccn.loc.gov/2023056269
LC ebook record available at https://lccn.loc.gov/2023056270)

Printed in the United States of America
Mankato, MN
082024

About the Author

Dalton Rains is a writer and editor from Minnesota.

Table of Contents

CHAPTER 1
Finding Food 5

CHAPTER 2
Body Parts 9

CHAPTER 3
Staying Safe 13

 THAT'S AMAZING!
Eyesight 16

CHAPTER 4
A Deer's Life 19

Focus on Deer • 22
Glossary • 23
To Learn More • 24
Index • 24

Chapter 1

Finding Food

A deer walks through a forest at **dusk**. It searches for food. Soon, it finds a clearing. The deer nibbles on grass. Then it hears a loud noise. It darts back into the forest.

Deer live together in **herds**. Many deer live in areas with forests, **meadows**, and farms. In the summer, they often stay in fields and meadows. In the winter, they stay in forests.

Fun Fact: Some deer **migrate** during winter. Others stay in one area. They sleep in thick bushes or under trees.

Chapter 2

Body Parts

Deer are **mammals**. They have fur all over their bodies. Deer have large ears. They have long, strong legs. They also have hooves on their feet.

Male deer are called bucks. Most bucks have antlers on their heads. Bucks lose their antlers every winter. In the spring, they start growing new ones.

Fun Fact

A deer's antlers can grow more than 1 inch (2.5 cm) every week.

Chapter 3

Staying Safe

Deer have **muscles** in their ears. The ears can turn in any direction. That helps deer hear well. They can hear **predators** coming.

Hooves protect a deer's feet. Hooves also help the deer move quietly. Strong legs help it run quickly. That way, it can get away from predators. A deer's fur is made of **hollow** hairs. The hairs keep the deer warm.

Fun Fact: Deer grow different colors of hair during different seasons. That way, they can blend in with nearby areas.

That's Amazing!

Eyesight

Deer cannot see very clearly during the day. But they can see well at dusk. Every deer has one eye on each side of its head. The deer can see almost all the way around its body. This helps the deer spot predators.

Chapter 4

A Deer's Life

Baby deer are called fawns. They are born during the spring. Female deer are called does. Mother does keep fawns hidden at first. Later, the fawns join the rest of the herd.

Male fawns stay with their mother for a year. After leaving, some form new herds. Females stay for two years. Most deer live for three to six years. Some can live up to 16 years.

Fun Fact

Male deer begin growing antlers the spring after they are born.

Life Cycle

FOCUS ON
Deer

Write your answers on a separate piece of paper.

1. Write a sentence describing where deer live.
2. Would you want a deer to live near your home? Why or why not?
3. How long do male fawns stay with their mother?
   - A. one year
   - B. two years
   - C. ten years
4. Why might having different colored fur help deer hide during different seasons?
   - A. Predators cannot see well during the summer.
   - B. Plants and trees change color depending on the season.
   - C. Fur makes deer warm during the winter.

Answer key on page 24.

Glossary

dusk
The time of day just before night when the sky gets dark.

herds
Groups of animals that stay together.

hollow
Having an empty space inside.

mammals
Animals that have hair and feed their babies milk.

meadows
Areas of land that are covered with grass.

migrate
To move from one place to another when the seasons change.

muscles
Parts of the body that help with strength and movement.

predators
Animals that hunt other animals for food.

To Learn More

BOOKS

Albertson, Al. *White-Tailed Deer.* Minneapolis: Bellwether Media, 2020.

Murray, Tamika M. *Meet a Baby White-Tailed Deer.* Minneapolis: Lerner Publications, 2024.

NOTE TO EDUCATORS

Visit **www.focusreaders.com** to find lesson plans, activities, links, and other resources related to this title.

Index

A
antlers, 10–11, 20–21

B
bucks, 11

D
does, 19

F
fawns, 19–21

H
herds, 7, 19–21

P
predators, 13–14, 16

Answer Key: **1.** Answers will vary; **2.** Answers will vary; **3.** A; **4.** B

i